THE
KINGDOM
ENTREPRENEUR

THE KINGDOM ENTREPRENEUR
THE 7 DAY BLUEPRINT

GOD'S PROVEN TEMPLATE

RYLEE MEEK

The Kingdom Entrepreneur Series
The Kingdom Entrepreneur: The 7 Day Blueprint
God's Proven Template

Copyright © 2022 by King's Council Media
All rights reserved.

ISBN: 979-8351751535

Editorial Management: Bruce Corris
Technical Editor | Layout | Cover Design: Kristin Watt

Unless otherwise noted, all scripture are from The ESV® Bible (The Holy Bible, English Standard Version®), copyright © 2001 by Crossway, a publishing ministry of Good News Publishers. Used by permission. All rights reserved.

Scripture marked NASB taken from the NEW AMERICAN STANDARD BIBLE®, Copyright © 1960,1962,1963,1968,1971,1972,1973,1975,1977,1995 by The Lockman Foundation. Used by permission.

Sale of this book without a front cover may be unauthorized. If this book is coverless, it may have been reported to the publisher as "unsold or destroyed" and neither the author nor the publisher has received payment for it.

No part of this publication may be reproduced, stored in a retrieval system, or transmitted in any form or by any means, electronic, mechanical, photocopying, recording, or otherwise, without the prior written permission of the Publisher. Requests to the Publisher for permission should be sent to King's Council Media, c/o 5888 Main Street, Suite 200, Williamsville, NY 14221.

Printed in the United States of America.

CONTENTS

Introduction – How to Use This Book	vii
CHAPTER ONE *Finding Abundance*	1
PART I – DISCOVER	13
CHAPTER TWO *DAY ONE – Establishing the Vision*	15
CHAPTER THREE *DAY TWO – Defining Your Atmosphere*	33
PART II – DEVELOP	47
CHAPTER FOUR *DAY THREE – Designing Your Structure*	49
CHAPTER FIVE *DAY FOUR – Determining Your Order*	65
PART III – DEPLOY	77
CHAPTER SIX *DAY FIVE – Gaining Momentum*	77

CHAPTER SEVEN
DAY SIX – Beginning to Multiply **89**

CHAPTER EIGHT
DAY SEVEN – Keeping the Sabbath **105**

CHAPTER NINE
A Final Word **113**

INTRODUCTION
HOW TO USE THIS BOOK

When I lead seminars or talk with people about the ideas in this book, I'm continually challenged to point out that while the subject is entrepreneurship and stewardship, the deeper value is learning what it means to live life in the "Kingdom Economy." I didn't coin this phrase, but in the businesses which I've started and helped to grow, this is the shared goal: to take our raw materials of work, connection, and faith, and steward them toward exponential growth.

There are specific biblical principles and practices I want to share that have helped us become successful. With so many active participants in this work, it's become more of a lifestyle for many of us, so there are stories I'd like to share about that as well. But mainly, I hope to give you a sense of what's possible if you will commit to God the resources that are His alone, and allow me to introduce you to this inspiring way to build on many of the ideas you probably already know, but just may not have fully lived out yet.

In full disclosure, this series may include some new thinking for you around the subject of successful work. But I promise, if you're familiar at all with the Bible's extensive teaching on money, you'll recognize many of the lessons and statements made here. The Kingdom Economy is about getting free of corporate-world thinking and acting, which I believe is a vestige of an old system of "servants and masters." More on that later. This series also includes much unoriginal content about biblical principles, including much from the prophets, Paul, Solomon, Jesus, and even God himself, and all of it is deep, good, and meaty. But it could easily be paraphrased and condensed into a much shorter book if not for the stories and application points that make the info hopefully go down more easily and memorably.

I've included "Main Takeaway" summaries at the start of each chapter. Then, at the end, you'll find application questions, and notes for any stats or studies mentioned. I encourage you not to skip these; they'll help the ideas take root and sprout, providing the fertile soil of *context* to fertilize your soul.

Finally, I want you to know I wrote this series after scouring Amazon and the business market for a resource that combined solid biblical principles on money and the Kingdom Economy, with simple story applications. Granted, that's pretty specific, but I couldn't find anything, so I reluctantly did what my heart was telling me and decided to capture my own experience in hopes it might be useful to someone. My hope and prayer is for some seasoned entrepreneurs to consider mentoring some young readers in learning and applying these ideas, and then pray, believing there will be some amazing results!

But most of all, I pray my family and friends who have supported me through all the ups and downs of this story will see their love and lessons reflected here and well invested. Because I believe that it's in making the wisest, most informed investments into others that we come to live the lives we've always wanted.

They know what it's taken for me to get to this point, and I think they'd agree there's no greater feeling than knowing all the struggle has been worth it.

CHAPTER ONE

FINDING ABUNDANCE

> **Main Takeaway:** *Finding abundance in our lives first means recognizing the fact that we not only have enormous resources at our disposal, we serve the King who owns the cattle on a thousand hills. God owns everything! This is why we need to begin to change our mindset about wealth as a resource.*

We all want to find abundance. I think this is why after a seminar or workshop, people often ask me, "Rylee, how did you do it? How did you manage to get where you are in life, leading and teaching from a place of abundance?" And because most of them know I'm a Christian, what I often hear them asking is, "How did you do all this *while being a Christian?*"

That mindset aggravates me, but I think I understand it. While there are plenty of Christians who have had phenomenal business success (think Walmart, Chick-fil-A, and Amway—all started by Christians), we tend to think making money is "worldly." So, if a company or a business is successful, that must mean the founders are a couple of steps below being "true Christians". After all, rich people can't be saved and saved people can't be rich, right?

Now to be clear, just because something makes a lot of money doesn't mean it's of excellence or good quality, much less "Christian." And if we're honest with each other, most Christian items seen in the marketplace often don't represent excellence. But this mindset coupled with the typical low-quality we've seen from Christian products and services is a bigger problem than we tend to realize. By and large, people are usually suspicious of Christian work, art, clothing, businesses…even Christian education…and for good reason. These days, anything with the name "Christian" attached to it has to work twice as hard to prove it isn't a second-rate copy of the "real" thing. I don't say this to shame or hurt anyone's feelings, but we have to be honest about this in order to address it. When compared to the world, Christian work often doesn't measure up, when in reality, we should be the most excellent creators on the planet, and produce the best quality products available. If, in fact, we are Christ's ambassadors, why aren't we operating this way?

Are we less intelligent? Of course not. From what I've seen, Christ-followers tend to be troubled about money. Besides maybe having a different definition of "excellence" and "success," I think a big part of our problem with money as Kingdom-minded people is our misunderstanding of finances in general. We tend to think it's not "Christian" to make money, and this idea took root a long time back. Much of it is unconscious and unexamined, so we need to reconsider how we tend to think about this and whether making money is actually unbiblical.

Does God hate money? Think about that. Is it true? Why do we think this? Maybe it's because we know loving money is a root of all kinds of evil. Yet as a resource, we know money is very important for getting things done in our world, perhaps second only to time. Maybe we need to realize the difference between loving money and using money responsibly. I think we need to consider what would happen if we stopped carrying around wrong ideas about God hating money and consider what we might see in the church as a result.

One of the reasons I wrote this series is because of the lack of financial abundance within the church when God gives us the blueprint and principles to acquire money and steward it well. There is nothing more frustrating than for a Kingdom Entrepreneur to see a need and not have the finances to fund that need. Especially when the needs we are talking about are a matter of life and death.

RICH CHRISTIANS

I also wrote this series for Christians to become more faithful with all the wealth they already have. The amount of money Christians currently possess is pretty astounding. 209 million Americans identify as Christian. 184.5 million are church members, and weekly attendance is 83 million, according to recent Pew Research and Gallup polls.[1] Yet of the nearly two-thirds of Americans who claim Christianity, only 10-25% say they "tithe" (about 15.5 million). The average amount is 2.5%, which isn't even close to 10%. It was 3.3% during the Great Depression.[2] American Christians are estimated to produce

---

[1] *https://news.gallup.com/poll/341963/church-membership-falls-below-majority-first-time.aspx*
[2] *https://nonprofitssource.com/online-giving-statistics/church-giving*

$5.2 trillion annually. 10% of that is $520 billion a year, or *38 times* what's currently given!

With $520 billion, all of the 380,000 churches in America could pay their average annual budget ($45.6 billion), and find room for a whole lot more. From an article published by the National Christian Foundation in 2019, here are just a few things churches could do with that 10% (inflation accounted for):

- $26.25 billion could relieve global hunger, starvation and deaths from preventable diseases in five years
- $12.6 billion could eliminate illiteracy in five years
- $15.75 billion could solve the world's water and sanitation issues, specifically at places in the world where one billion people live on less than $1 per day
- $1.1 billion could fully fund all overseas mission work

And there's still over $418.7 billion left over! Imagine the kind of kingdom impact we could have with that kind of investment.

Bear in mind, this is just simple math. Imagine what God could supernaturally do on top of our natural efforts. Since we can influence peoples' hearts and convictions, I believe the quickest, most impactful way to be the change is to make people aware of this situation. From there, I'm hopeful we'll see more Christians supporting Christian businesses and learning to steward that growth into greater generosity, even beyond the 10% standard.

Because here's the thing: whether or not you agree tithing is biblical, when we begin to sow into Kingdom-focused businesses, the God of multiplication could begin to blow our minds. Say one person makes $100 and tithes $10. If they spend the other $90 at Christian businesses, their tithe will be $9 total from that. If other Christian businesses received that $81, they'd tithe $8 total, and on and on, building the kingdom in our midst. I'm not advising to spend 90% of your paychecks, but using this to illustrate a point. I believe money can do one of two things: it can be controlled (saved/invested) or consumed (spent).

In this scenario, the church could pay their staff, who then tithe back, and hire Christian vendors who also tithe. You can see how this very elementary approach would build the Kingdom Economy like nothing else. Of course, a Christian business directory for every product and service is needed and we have one in the works. But until then I'll bet you have a personal mental list of Christians who offer various items and things you purchase. So just imagine if we all pooled our resources and worked toward this achievable dream of investing in the Kingdom Economy together.

That's basically what I want to explore in this book and the rest of this series. I want to look at what that might mean for you, and how I've experienced Kingdom thinking taking shape and root in my own life. In each chapter, I include some of my successes and failures to show what I think we need to do to improve our own financial abundance, and understand the *real* biblical principles for kingdom investing.

Over the course of my life, I have seen God prepare me to recognize this problem and speak this message. Personally, with those I've helped in the businesses they've founded, it's been nothing short of life-changing to see what God has done. I've been so eager to share what I discovered over the past few years, so beyond telling the story at conferences and on my podcast to anyone who will listen, I'm excited to finally capture all of this in a book you can read and share with others.

Now let's get down to business!

THE KING'S COUNCIL METHOD

I built The King's Council "method" on the seven days of creation, as they're written in the Book of Genesis. Whether we see these as literal or figurative days doesn't matter for our purposes as much as recognizing the sequence and order of each day. Taken as seven distinct steps, I believe it's important to appreciate not just the fact that God created our reality, but *the way* He did it and how that can quickly help improve our understanding of the process for building any enterprise.

I often call it a "strategy" as well, or even a "system". It's not something I own and I don't have a patent on the idea, I just believe it's a way to think broadly about what we're yearning to achieve and why, which then helps structure *how* we go about it. I talk specifically on how these steps apply to business, but in reality, this God-given blueprint can and should be applied to whatever we are creating, whether that be a new relationship, an incredible marriage, or a successful business. Once you understand the concepts behind each step, you'll see how this can apply in so many ways. I hope you'll find many of your own applications for it after going through my quick explanation here.

God's Word contains creative power and the playbook to creating fruitful relationships, successful businesses, and a fulfilling life. The first thing God reveals about Himself in Scripture is **not** that He is holy, all-knowing, omnipotent, loving, gracious, or even just. What I find fascinating is that God shows us that He is creative! In Genesis, God creates! It says the earth was formless and empty, and from the darkness, He spoke and created, not just for Himself, but for the good of others!

This insight into God's power, and how He uses it, is very instructive to entrepreneurs. Think about what it means that even before there was anything, there was God's creativity. This is the reason we ought to be very respectful of that creative impulse that arises out of our built-in hardware. Each of us carries the image of God, and because of that, we have access to this source of inspiration to fuel and drive our ideas to their greatest fulfillment.

But as subjects of the High King, we have a great responsibility and a great advantage over our competition in seeing the greatest motivation for all creativity. It's in God's very nature to create for the good of all people. Not self-focused or dependent on anything or anyone else, God put us first as the pinnacle of his creation to serve and delight us through his incredible provision. If you provide goods and services, you are this kind of provider and server. You can tap into this knowledge when you set out, and when you face decisions in your work.

For six days, God created. Then, on the seventh day, He rested. However, there is one important thing to take note of that God did every day of the six days. Each day "God said" and what he called for — became. Other scriptures support the literalness of this. It's inspiring to think how powerful our words are in changing reality, but remember, this is because we're drawing that power from a deep source. Again, *responsibility and advantage.* It's both.

We're going to break this down and learn to apply God's Word on creation in three major sections or phases of this awesome power of creativity:

Discover,

Develop,

Deploy.

Each of these phases is described in two steps apiece, which God separated by defining as "days." Taken together, God's method of dividing up the work of creation is something of a divine blueprint for all creation and human enterprise.

As a quick overview, in the discovery phase, there's the need to first define the *vision* (day one), and then the *atmosphere* or culture of your business (day two). The development phase includes days three, on creating the *structure*, and four, establishing the *order* of business operations. Finally, in the deployment phase, day five is about gaining *momentum* in those operations, and day six, *multiplying* the relationships and goodness we've included. Taken together, these six considerations help ensure our businesses and methods are excellent, and our systems for creating, delivering, and adjusting over time are as well.

Day Seven, of course, is a model to *rest* from our labors, and this is where we'll *reflect* honestly on how our business is going. In a competitive environment, this step is arguably a Kingdom entrepreneur's greatest advantage over those who would simply plow forward with substandard products and try to overwhelm the market by sheer unrelenting force. Maybe that works for a time, but it doesn't help fulfill the customer's deeper need with a higher-quality product.

The seventh day of creation is just as important as the other six — rest is as important as work. We'll cover that in its own chapter since it's a hidden key to productivity and success no Kingdom entrepreneur can afford to neglect.

Now, as followers of the Almighty Creator, let's use the strategy found in God's Word to level up and take territory for His Kingdom!

PART I

DISCOVER

In the beginning God created the heavens and the earth. The earth was without form, and void; and darkness was on the face of the deep. And the Spirit of God was hovering over the face of the waters. - Genesis 1:1-2

Phase one of the seven-day method is "Discover" which involves two steps, or days.

Days one and two are about discovering what God's call means for us and how we might best respond to that effectively.

In any large undertaking, before developing and deploying, we must take the time to slow down and consider the full opportunity before us.

CHAPTER TWO

DAY ONE
ESTABLISHING THE VISION

And God said, "Let there be light," and there was light. And God saw that the light was good. And he separated the light from the darkness. God called the light Day, and the darkness he called Night. And there was evening and there was morning, the first day. (Genesis 1:3-5).

*And the L*ORD *answered me: "Write the vision; make it plain on tablets, so he may run who reads it"* (Habakkuk 2:2).

> **Main Takeaway:** *God supplies the vision. We must learn to see it and practice the habits that get us there.*

Who do you want to become? Now, I'm a firm believer in the truth that we are already exactly who we need to be, and when Jesus comes into your life, he can activate and awaken those things created in you to share. But the work of becoming who we truly are often involves dispelling false notions of ourselves that we and others believe.

The first thing God did was He dispelled darkness. That is, He cast His vision. For you, "dispelling darkness" might involve helping your customer or client recognize the promise of what you're offering, the "light of hope." That might sound grandiose or strange, but this foundation is important, and a basic tool of every entrepreneur, to help people find hope to move forward, get unstuck, or make progress toward beginning something new in their lives. From the basic paper clip to a vacation cruise to learning a new language, everyone wants to know or do that new thing that's going to improve their life, and an entrepreneur is someone who makes that happen in some way, using some great product or service.

That's what I want to help you do. What I often see happening with people who dream of helping others in this way with some great new idea, is they lose steam and momentum when they don't know how to sustain that dream over the long term as setbacks and failures happen and the months drag on. They go from being an enhancer of others' dreams to being a barrier to them just to stay afloat. Pretty soon they're not offering much of value to help people thrive. They're mostly *taking* things of value from others in order to survive.

A few years back, God revealed to me why I continually experienced disappointment amidst failures and even what many would call success over the years, these extreme highs and lows that kept happening in my life. It was because I wasn't truly rooted in Him. My mission (how), vision (what), and purpose (why) in life wasn't clear. It wasn't until I established my core values and true identity in who He says I am, not what I or even others say I am, that I was able to get clear on my vision.

Then, once I got around the right people (atmosphere) I was able to put the proper structure in my life that led to implementation (order) that ultimately has created momentum - a rhythm that allows me to multiply, go forth, and take dominion. The last step is always the commitment to taking time to rest and honor God by reflecting on everything that He has done and continues to do in my life.

WHAT IS VISION?

Vision is *not* a goal. A goal is *something* you want to accomplish, while vision is *someone* you want to be. Before you can set up an atmosphere (day two) or spend time creating the structure (day three), you must spend time defining the vision of who you are or who you want to become.

In order to get to the root of a person's want, keep asking why. Too many people just start working and hope they become a millionaire, failing to think through their vision for the future.

This was me, early on. My family was deeply involved in the network marketing company Herbalife, so naturally I got involved too. But I didn't have any idea what kind of a lifestyle I wanted or what I wanted life to look like.

Once your million is in the bank, do you have a vision for how you'd like life to look to ensure you talk to your spouse regularly, or spend your mornings in the most productive way? I wish someone had asked me this sooner: *What does it feel like to be the guy or gal you imagine as successful?* Having vision forms our daily habits and the patterns we create from what we value.

BEFORE CREATION

The first thing God did was dispel darkness. Translation: On day one, God cast His **vision.** When God said, "Let there be light," light appeared as a thing separate from darkness. The phrase *let there be light* could be confusing to some, as if God was asking for light instead of declaring that is should happen.

The phrase *let there be light* is a translation of the Hebrew phrase *yehi 'or*, which was translated "*fiat lux*" in Latin. A literal translation would be a command, something like, "Light, exist." God is speaking into the void and commanding light to come into being. Genesis 1 tells us that God created the heavens and the earth and everything else that exists by simply speaking them into existence. The idea of light existed first in God's mind and was given form by the words "Let there be light" ("Let light exist").

In 1 John 1:5, we read that "God *is* light." This means God began the creation process of the universe by extending *Himself,* sending His energy out. Taken simply at face value, everything that exists is made of light, including water, and scientists confirm that the universe is still expanding at the speed of light.

My point is, God had a massive, infinitely complex vision for what He wanted to create, and His words, based in His beliefs, spoke it to life. For our purposes, your vision for your business will be based in a well-developed mental picture of the life you want to lead.

GOALS, HABITS, AND MINDSETS

Everything you eventually produce will be created from this vision, so you must determine what you want and how it should look. I started this book by pointing out our unhealthy relationship with money, because understanding the big problem is key to knowing what's needed to solve it. In Proverbs, we learn, *"Where there is no vision, the people are unrestrained, but happy is one who keeps the Law"* (29:18, NASB). What we need first is a bigger vision for our lives than simply making money.

In network marketing you have to go to your family and friends to get them to join. I did that, but my friends and family had all either drunk the Kool-Aid already and were in it, or they hated it. The company told us we simply needed to talk to more people and then ask if they wanted to join. But that didn't work for me. I knew I needed a way to get people to call *me*. I eventually came up with an idea, which I'll share more about later, but my whole mindset was around making money at the time, so it wasn't sustainable.

Making money or even having a great business is a goal. Again, not a vision. But in order to obtain a proper vision for our life we first need to look at our *mindset*. Who we are is largely based on the mindsets we've adopted. If you grew up witnessing that money was hard to come by, or that men are all pigs, or that religion is destructive or boring, that will be your mindset. Maybe you learned that rich people are bad or poor people are lazy. If you know how someone grew up, often it's no wonder why they believe what they do. Once we understand this, life can be a struggle to unlearn many wrong beliefs.

Your vision is not a "goal" but more of a mindset established by a series of habits of healthy thoughts and intentional actions you develop. Goals can help you get to where you're going, but goals are not the same as having a clear vision of what you want. Goals are great stepping stones for working out your vision and developing the habits that are essential to keep you on track.

Because our mindsets are largely unsolicited gifts from our parents, teachers, and society, each of us is the product of other people's habitual ways of thinking, just as they were, and those before them. But when we uncritically accept these values, beliefs, and habits, they will have a strong control over our lives. When considering our mindsets, it's important to understand that we create them, therefore, we can change them or build new ones. Studies actually prove that we can build new neuropathways.[3]

Think of your mindset like a jungle. Imagine you're standing in the middle of it and you notice a path that has been forged. You realize that over time, that path was created because of all the times people walked it. As you look over to the left you notice what seems to be a path less traveled. Few people have ever taken it. It's full of brush and can be hard to follow initially, but the more you take it, the easier it will become to find and follow. Our mindsets are made the same way.

An entrepreneur is one who endeavors to take a different path, who starts cutting a new trail for others and your

---

[3] *https://cedwardpitt.com/2017/05/22/dr-caroline-leaf-and-the-power-of-prayer*

family to follow. For most people who take this path, it's a chance to have the legacy they believe they were designed for. Of course, changing your mindset doesn't happen in a day. It takes time to build new habits. In order to destroy old habits, thought patterns, and mindsets—to *dispel the darkness*—you have to keep pouring light in. New habits create new neural pathways, so it's important to note that this doesn't happen overnight. It happens over time. It's a process.

We have to consider several key areas that indicate what we need, primarily surrounding yourself with the right people, getting the right input, and learning to hear what your language says, both internally and externally. Slowly, as you do these things, your mindset will begin to change. We'll look more closely at who we choose in Day Two, "Designing Your Atmosphere." But for now, consider just how important what you think is in what you believe, and the actions you take. This is why we must start with our mindsets and develop the proper vision for what we want to cast into the world.

Remember Paul's guidance on changing mindsets in Philippians 4:8-9, "Finally, brothers and sisters, whatever is true, whatever is honorable, whatever is right, whatever is pure, whatever is lovely, whatever is commendable, if there is any excellence and if anything is worthy of praise, think about such things. As for the things you have learned and received and heard and seen in me, practice these things, and the God of peace will be with you" (NASB). As we make the effort to consider these things in our lives—the people, opportunities, and situations we'd describe this way—eventually we can be assured our habits of thought will change. Again, it's a continual process of thinking about those things, and then putting your thoughts into practice, trusting that the God of peace goes with us.

YOUR VISION GIVES PAIN PURPOSE

So, what we need to figure out is *how* exactly to do this. Changing our thoughts and practices is what we have to get clear on, because more than anything else, your ***vision gives pain purpose.***

When I was 16, I was introduced to this concept of "knowing your why." I was taught to have big goals, so big that I would do whatever it takes to accomplish it. I would endure the pain. When I decided to commit to working out, I was reintroduced to this. I had to be willing to endure the pain to obtain the stronger, healthier body I desired. I felt I had a grasp on this but only when I realized what Christ did for me did I fully come to understand the importance of vision.

Back when I was selling supplements with Herbalife, I did okay and made some decent money. But it wasn't until I decided I wanted more that I first had to figure out how hard I was willing to work. I was starting to understand marketing, and while I never had any formal education in it, I realized people don't buy what they need, they buy what they want. As much as everybody needs good nutrition and exercise for good health, they don't want it. So, I thought, "How can I get them to want this?" I came up with an ad and put it in the back pages of the Pennysavers, and literally all it said was "We pay you to lose weight," with an 800 number that forwarded to the phone in my little rented office.

Well, my phone started ringing off the hook, which made me think, "Okay, now I have to figure out how to present to these people." I ended up building out a program with three levels—good, better, and best—and I started to get feedback from people about what their objections were. I incorporated it and things began to take off. That was one of my initial lessons in the principle that people will let you sell them anything if it's something they really want.

But all of this started with a vision, and admittedly not much else. I had much to learn yet, but I knew the basics, at least the first step. It would take me several years to finally stop and consider how the vision God originally had for the world applied to my vision for my business. It would take even longer to see how through the cross Jesus was teaching us endurance through struggle and pain. Eventually, I wondered, *How did He endure it all?* The Bible says, "For the joy set before Him." He could persist through the pain, face it head-on, even though it was unbearable in the moment, to say the least. Jesus could do this because He focused on the redemption of the original vision God created.

It blows my mind to think that through the pain He was thinking of me and you, and that His love for us was the driving force to persevere. So, whatever you're facing today, I want you to know that your Father in heaven is looking at you with love in His eyes and compassion in His heart. He can empathize and connect with your pain because He felt it all on the cross. As you develop your vision, take heart in knowing that my vision has changed drastically over the years. As we mature and grow in faith, our vision comes more in alignment with His. Just take the next step to walk out, Matthew 6:33, and know it's the small daily things we do that continually bring us to greater clarity.

Remember also Philippians 3:12-14: "Not that I have already obtained all this, or have already arrived at my goal, but I press on to take hold of that for which Christ Jesus took hold of me. Brothers and sisters, I do not consider myself yet to have taken hold of it. But one thing I do: Forgetting what is behind and straining toward what is ahead, I press on toward the goal to win the prize for which God has called me heavenward in Christ Jesus" (NASB). Press on toward that goal with the vision to win the prize for which God has called you heavenward in Christ Jesus!

Again, I want to be clear that I don't mean vision as merely "sight," but as deeper insight. When God created light in the darkness, He didn't need to see anything, but we know from scripture that He created what originated first in His mind, and then He spoke it into being. And of course, since He is God, He knew full well that sin would ultimately threaten to destroy His creation, and that He would have to send his Son, Jesus, to redeem us. But His vision gave that pain He felt, even in the first moments, a higher purpose.

"And the light shines in the darkness, and the darkness did not comprehend it" (John 1:5 NKJV).

This deeper vision we want starts in our minds. Regardless of the experiences and situations we've faced, this is how we each get to create our reality. Consider how you've spent your life creating the one you presently have based largely on your beliefs. Life is determined by and even co-created by your perception, and it can change the moment you choose to change it. Like God instructed Habakkuk, we need to write the vision He gives and make it plain so we know how to live.

Our core beliefs are the foundation every believer needs to overcome their limits and run their race.

CHANGE THE CHANNEL

Think of a bad vision as a bad TV show. We've all watched a bad show where about halfway though you think, "What the heck am I watching?" You realize it's a terrible program, so what do you do? Do you smash the TV? Certainly not. You simply change the channel and choose something better, more your style.

When we change our thoughts, we change our results. It's one of the few places in life we can see a simple cause and effect. As we begin to practice continually thinking about what Philippians 4:8 suggests, our perspective changes, our conscious thoughts become more subconscious, and our subconscious begins to affect every cell of our body and change us from the inside out. Science is just catching up with what the wisdom of the aged already suspected and understood.

Have you ever been driving only to find yourself pulling into your driveway as you snap out of it and think to yourself, *How did I get here?* Our subconscious controls most of what our bodies do on a regular basis. You don't have to consciously make an effort. If I had to think about every little part of the process just to move my arm, it would be impossible. God created us this way. Once we learn where all the keys are on the keyboard, eventually over time our subconscious is able to take over. The results people have experienced from hypnotism and behavior therapy prove that what we hold as true in our subconscious changes our reality. There is something very powerful and important about what we believe.

Knowing this is the first step in changing our lives for the better, and this is why it's so important to choose our thoughts wisely. As it says in Romans 12:2, "Do not be conformed to this world, but be transformed by the renewal of your mind, that by testing you may discern what is the will of God, what is good and acceptable and perfect." I think most of us can read that verse and not quite understand that Paul is essentially saying, "Yes! Your mind can be completely transformed!"

LET GOD GROW YOUR VISION

God has a *plan,* a *purpose*, a *dream,* and a *vision* for your life, so start making the rest of your life the best of your life! Helen Keller said, *"The most pathetic person in the world is someone who has sight but has no vision."* Dare to dream big, and get clear on your broader vision. If you're struggling to know what that is, ask God to give you a God-sized vision—for your faith, marriage, kids, finances, character, and everything else you choose to have in your life. If you really want to jump-start your adventure, start diving into the Word regularly and watch God grow your vision.

You can see how eventually this process of considering your proper vision applies to your business and how you're making money. But it doesn't stop there. Like anything we build in life, a solid business is the direct result of a solid life that's been well considered, shaped, and tended. Once we get clear on this process and know how to discover a solid vision, we can move on to Day Two and explore what defines our atmosphere and culture.

CHAPTER THREE

DAY TWO
DEFINING YOUR ATMOSPHERE

And God said, "Let there be an expanse in the midst of the waters, and let it separate the waters from the waters." And God made the expanse and separated the waters that were under the expanse from the waters that were above the expanse. And it was so. And God called the expanse Heaven. And there was evening and there was morning, the second day. (Genesis 1:6-8)

Whoever walks with the wise becomes wise, but the companion of fools will suffer harm." Proverbs 13:20)

> **Main Takeaway:** *Just as God established the atmosphere to create the context for life, we need to define our business culture to create the context for success.*

Everything in this book is powerful, but only if implemented. It's been said that knowledge is power, but I wholeheartedly disagree. Knowledge *applied* is power. That being said, this chapter's wisdom is straight-up some of the best biblical insight I've found, and I hope and pray all my family and friends will come to deeply understand it. Just imagining how my 10-year-old daughter can use this and benefit inspires me like nothing else. I want to hand her the keys to this new way of thinking so she's prepared and knows how to live with abundance well invested. This is absolutely the plan I hope she'll have, far better than anything I had just starting out.

So, start here: God's Word created the firmament (some versions say "vault" or "expanse," verse 6). This is the atmosphere and air space. Notice once again that God accomplished His work simply by speaking the word. When God speaks, life, order, goodness, and all good things emerge!

Isaiah 55:10-11 says God's Word will accomplish what He sent it forth to do. Deuteronomy says "Man lives by every word that comes from the mouth of the Lord" (8:3). The Psalms say God has magnified His Word above His name and Paul says it performs its work in those who believe (1 Thess.

2:13). Man is born again through God's Word (1 Pet.1:23), which is not merely the Bible, or even the Old Testament "statutes" and "decrees." God's Word is Jesus and also His original creative power.

God's Word is the greatest power in the universe. We must learn to base our lives on it and it alone.

On the second day of creation week, God continued His work of preparing the earth so plants could grow in it, and animals and people could live on it. God called the expanse the "heaven," which we call sky. God separated the water above the earth from the water on the earth, placing the sky between the two. The sky (our atmosphere) is like a blanket of gases which protects the earth. Because of the atmosphere, the sun does not burn us to death and we do not freeze at night when the sun sets. Although we cannot see the atmosphere, it is constantly playing the part that God intended it to play.

God didn't create land until the third day, so air and water were the original "elements" for a while all on their own. When you think how water is made up of two basic elements, both of which are two of the most abundant things in our world—hydrogen and oxygen—you see there's more to this idea of atmosphere than it seems at first glance. Hydrogen combines to form other very common compounds (from ammonia, to methane, to table sugar, to hydrogen peroxide and hydrochloric acid), and oxygen is the most common element in the earth. Experts estimate that 90% of what we can see in the universe is made up of hydrogen, and half of the earth's crust is made of oxygen (the land, dirt, and rocks part, not just the water).[4]

Hydrogen and oxygen are involved in most matter that exists—every object in the universe—and we can neither create it nor destroy it, only change their forms in limited ways. Think of how clouds form from water vapor in the air, and how wind carries this evaporated water to different areas. Or think of how ice forms when temperatures drop and it becomes a solid that creates surfaces and "land-like" structures in the form of icebergs and great ice shelves. New things are created when these elements undergo chemical changes and form new bonds with other elements.

Like us, these elements are products of their environments, so if we want to change what we do and even

---

[4] *https://education.nationalgeographic.org/resource/conservation-matter-during-physical-and-chemical-changes*

who we are, we need to consider our environments and our bonds.

So now that we have that context, for our purposes what does a biblical "atmosphere" look like?

WHAT IS ATMOSPHERE?

This is another lesson it took me a long time to learn, but in your business, you determine the atmosphere and culture. You set the tone for the way you conduct your business, and this is the feeling of the place you spend much of your time each day. Ask a simple question: Does your atmosphere match your vision? Do the people you surround yourself with support the vision you have created? As a leader, you need to be a resource to them, and be resourceful in your dealings.

Remember that ad I ran offering to pay people to lose weight? I ran it as a six-week program because I knew they would have to buy at least two months of my product to do the regimens, and though I'd pay them per pound or per inch they lost, they would usually just use their credit toward more product. While I found myself at the age of 19 retailing over $10,000 a month in vitamins and nutritional supplements, which was great, I was working my tail off, up to 16-18 hours a day, meeting one-on-one and also trying to run a fitness training business, so I had zero lifestyle. Also, I knew what I was doing was not duplicatable. It couldn't be replicated to invite others to go through this process. There was still that itch to find something more sustainable and shareable. Plus, as great as it was to be making money, I didn't have anyone to share it with because I didn't have any infrastructure.

What kind of atmosphere you have in your business will determine much of what you produce, and who you choose to work with has much bearing on this. You can work as hard as you want with those around you, but if they are not the right people helping you get into the right situations, you will find yourself getting further and further away from your vision.

Although you can't see the atmosphere, it is very important. In our physical world, our atmosphere is the air we breathe and the space we inhabit. All life needs it. Our air is made up of nitrogen, oxygen, and a tiny amount of other gases such as carbon dioxide. These are in just the right amounts for our survival. If there were a little more of any one element, a spark could set the world on fire or we would suffocate.

Carbon dioxide is deadly to humans in large quantities. We need to strive for a near-perfect balance to survive and thrive.

Similarly, your business, your marriage, your family all need a proper balance of vital elements. What's the atmosphere like in your marriage, your family, your business? God spoke everything into existence and nothing that exists can be created or destroyed; only reshaped or remade.

WHAT IS A *HEALTHY* ENVIRONMENT OR CULTURE?

I have a podcast episode about influencing our environments for good where I asked, "Are you the thermostat or are you the thermometer?" Are you the one who lets life happen to you, becoming a reflection of what's going on around you in your environment? Or are you the kind of person who's able to adjust the temperature around you, someone who doesn't immediately conform to the environment you're in just to fit in or get by? Are you an "affecter" or someone who's affected by everything around you? A thermometer only shows what's going on in the atmosphere around us. But a thermostat regulates and changes the atmosphere, exerting control over what you decide it should be.

When I look back at my life and career, it's crystal clear to me that any time I leveled up, it was because I put myself in a new circle. I was so intentional about who I was surrounding myself with. Most people take this for granted. But hear me when I say this: opportunity is built on your accessibility, and not on your ability. Your accessibility is what matters.

So, what do I mean by that? You have greatness inside of you. I know that because Greatness Himself created you and the Bible says that we are made in his image. Therefore, we have greatness inside of us. That being said, that seed of greatness needs to take root. The determinant of that seed ever taking root is dependent on what it's surrounded with. Are you surrounding yourself with people that are going to allow that greatness to thrive? Are you putting yourself in the right environments?

It's been said a baby shark or a goldfish will stay small in a small tank, but can grow much larger in the ocean. It actually has more to do with the quality of the water and its space to thrive, but there can be a massive difference in the health of the shark or the fish depending on their environment, and that's just how powerful your atmosphere is affecting you.[5]

The point is, a shark or fish (or any animal) will never be healthier than its environment, and the same is true about you. If you want to grow and thrive as a contributing member of your community, your growth and progress depend upon your environment.

If you look around at your closest group of friends, your closest circle of people, and you're not inspired, you are not in a circle. You're in a cage and it's time to level up. You don't necessarily have to shun those people, but you do need to find another group to glean from.

Romans 12:2 says, *"Do not be conformed to this world, but be transformed by the renewal of your mind, that by testing you may discern what is the will of God, what is good and acceptable and perfect."* Very simply: we're not meant to conform to our environments, we're meant to transform them. If you want your work to have kingdom impact for generations, you have to establish a culture of health and vitality that's based in these biblical principles of

---

[5] *https://www.tfhmagazine.com/articles/freshwater/goldfish-myths-debunked*

grace, love, and excellence. You have to get granular and specific about who you're with and what they're bringing. That means at every point you need to seek God's wisdom about who to invest in, and who to separate from. There will be some difficult conversations that focus on better aligning on these kingdom values. Always with grace, and always with the most patient love, but with a dogged dedication to keeping God and His values first.

CREATING KINGDOM CULTURE

Everyone needs a Paul, a Barnabas, and a Timothy in life. This familiar saying carries a pretty simple meaning, but when applied, it can be transformative. Basically, everyone needs a mentor, an associate, and an apprentice. Someone to build into our lives, someone to labor alongside us, and someone to help and pass along God's timeless wisdom and knowledge to. We likely need more than one person in each of these categories, and often we won't know who's leading and who's learning from whom. However, the principle is sound.

Timothy 2:2 says, "And what you have heard from me in the presence of many witnesses entrust to faithful men, who will be able to teach others also." Paul invested a significant amount of time and energy into Timothy, and now Timothy was instructed to do the same with other men. The Bible is full of gospel partnerships. In Acts, we see how Paul teamed up with Barnabas, and then later with Silas and others. As gifted as Paul was, he was never a one-man show. He worked side-by-side with hundreds of people, like Barnabas.

Do you have a Paul, a Barnabas, and a Timothy in your life? If you don't, you're not alone. Don't get discouraged; start praying about it and begin considering who comes to mind as you reflect on those categories in your life. Then follow up and ask who God lays on your heart, expecting there to be some friction, even some resistance. You're looking for someone who recognizes the value of this, the serious time investment involved, and the limits of our busy, modern lives. You should also be prepared to let your assumptions about those categories be tested. I've learned much from people I thought were merely associates or mentees, and mentors have become partners I've even been able to encourage and advise at times.

But be hopeful in this ongoing search and don't be afraid to share and seek out what you need and hope for from others. If you're willing to listen and grow, you'll find that the type of relationship you had in mind was exactly what they were looking for too!

And from your *alignments* will birth your *assignments*. If you don't know what's next or what to do, align yourself with likeminded people—people of a similar mindset—and your assignment will be birthed. If you're on assignment right now, that's great! It's time to align yourself with people of the same mindset.

Recently, I heard this illustration from Bill Gosling about healthy work culture.[6] He said there are four main things we can take from geese, and specifically how they fly in a V formation. First, by flying behind other geese to reduce wind resistance, the flock can fly 70% further than flying solo. They might go faster solo, but they go farther *together*. They also rotate the lead role to allow time for each to rest. They honk at each other to communicate fatigue and encourage the lead, demonstrating that accountability and encouragement go hand in hand. Geese also bond and help each other when one gets injured or sick, staying together until the weaker one can rejoin the rest.

---

[6] *https://www.billgosling.com/blog/5-things-geese-can-teach-you-about-teamwork*

So, who are you flying with? Who are you doing life with? Remember, opportunity is built not on your ability but on your *accessibility*. Are you making yourself accessible? God knew the importance of this, so He provided many models to show us. But the atmosphere we put ourselves in, as well as the atmosphere we are creating in our home lives and businesses is the best indicator of our future success.

PART II

DEVELOP

"Go to the ant, you sluggard; consider its ways and be wise! It has no commander, no overseer or ruler, yet it stores its provisions in summer and gathers its food at harvest." – Proverbs 6:6-8

"Chance favors the prepared mind." – Louis Pasteur

The goal of this section is to help you take time to think about what your business will need, research the competition, consider options, get outside opinions, and create a structure and order that's efficient, streamlined, and flexible to the market and unforeseen circumstances.

CHAPTER FOUR

DAY THREE
DESIGNING YOUR STRUCTURE

And God said, "Let the waters under the heavens be gathered together into one place, and let the dry land appear." ...And God said, "Let the earth sprout vegetation, plants yielding seed, and fruit trees bearing fruit in which is their seed, each according to its kind, on the earth." And it was so. ... And God saw that it was good. And there was evening and there was morning, the third day. (Genesis 1:9, 11-13)

But all things should be done decently and in order. (1 Corinthians 14:40)

> **Main Takeaway:** *Structure defines what operations are needed and what tasks are involved to ensure your business runs smoothly.*

The framework of the seven days was first suggested to me by a mentor as "God's blueprint" for our lives. It took me a while to appreciate it, but once I dove in and started applying it, I realized there was way more to it. I saw how Day One, Vision, related to the power of our words, and I started thinking about how to apply this to our context. I wondered why we should even care about this for our lives. As I discussed this with others, and as I saw myself getting out of sequence, I knew I needed a better understanding of the playbook.

Somewhere I got the idea to go back to the beginning and read Genesis. All I knew was I needed to get myself, and my life, in order. My relationship and business struggles showed my lack of a plan, so I could tell I needed discipline to first slow down and start evaluating what I was doing wrong. When I came upon the God-given blueprint right in the beginning of the Bible, it seemed obvious this framework had to be for something greater than myself. Soon it dawned on me that this was a model for building a better, more ordered life. Over time, God showed me how the sequence of creation could apply to literally everything that really matters in life—love, work, school, time, finances, and relationships.

When I was a kid, I knew I needed more than I'd had. Even as a young man I knew this. I'll never forget how exciting it felt to remember a moment God revealed to me when I was young, a vision of myself that I would be very successful one day. I gained some early success too, so it was very confirming to me, and I believe that memory from childhood set me on a course of success. More than once it has kept me from giving up after a big failure.

Case in point, this story. When I was 20 and still working in network marketing, I had the opportunity to partake in a company expansion into Malaysia. It was the usual pitch of "a ground-floor opportunity" with huge upside for minimal investment. I had big ambitions, but not much of a plan, and I ended up having a panic attack from culture shock after being there only one day. I lost significant time, money, and confidence trying to hurry things along on my own, but by God's grace, I got back home and that set the stage for learning one of the most valuable lessons of my life. Before that trip, I had no idea what I was missing. But soon I saw I needed a better support structure for my big ideas and dreams.

My *real* ground-floor opportunity was staring me in the face. It was in becoming more *available* to God.

This is when things really started to take off for me. My trouble before was, as I said, I didn't have a structure or appreciate the order of things or the core value of *availability*. I was just trying new idea after new idea to make money. I've since learned from experience that God gives to us more according to our ability, which is made up of three things: Our availability, the responsibility we are willing to take on, and the accountability we are willing to have in our life. The parable of the talents provides one of the best lessons in how we can increase, and when I say how God gave to me according to my ability, it's clear looking back on why I had so many highs and lows in my different business endeavors. I didn't know what was wrong, and it wasn't until I started making myself more available to God and meditated on what He values and His created order that I started really growing.

On the third day of creation, God formed the Earth. There are two specific things God accomplished on Day Three. One is the separation of land from the waters, and the second was creating vegetation. These weren't random acts. This was deliberate organization for the continuance of life. The water God gathered together, he called seas; and within each form of vegetation he put seeds, "each according to its kind." Life as we can recognize it began on Day Three "and God saw that it was good." Translation: God created *structure*.

WHAT IS STRUCTURE?

A structure is merely the support for something you build, so it's easy to undervalue. But once you have your vision and you understand what your surroundings involve and what atmosphere you want to have, it's time to get a plan down on paper for what your structure will look like and begin creating it.

We were all created to create—that's God-given. But so many people look for and fulfill that desire in less meaningful pursuits. A common definition of entrepreneurship could be where self-driven individuals participate in a free market economy, for the purpose of controlling resources and *creating* wealth to further their interests. I define "Kingdom entrepreneurship" as exercising God-given dominion and stewardship over God's resources, to serve others profitably and *create* benefit for the Kingdom of God. I see the seven-day sequence as a primary blueprint for creating or building anything—financial, personal, or relational. In a very real way, we can see God as the first creative "entrepreneur" giving us a blueprint on how to operate as "creatives" in the world.

Earlier I pointed out that the first thing God reveals about Himself in Scripture is that He is creative. In Genesis, He brings something out of nothing and order out of chaos, and creates for the good of others. I would submit that an entrepreneur is anyone who takes a risk to create something new for the good of others.

BECOMING DISCIPLINED ENTREPRENEURS

The word originally meant "to undertake," but "entrepreneur" is a title thrown around so much today, it has become difficult to pin down. Using the idea that entrepreneurship is risking creating something for the good of others, I believe the Creator of the universe certainly qualifies as the first entrepreneur. In Genesis, He is clearly creating something new for others that's risky. Before creation, we're told "the earth was formless and empty" until the first entrepreneur spoke. Then, in six days, His voice brought forth the heavens, the earth, light, evening, morning, sky, land, sea, vegetation, sun, moon, stars, animals, and man.

Following in the footsteps of the original entrepreneur, we are called to create. So often, we think of work as a curse—as something God made us do *after* we got kicked out of the Garden. But what if work is actually a part of His image? What if it's an invitation to create and build alongside the ultimate entrepreneur? What if work is something God gave us as a vehicle through which we can enjoy His presence? I'd like to suggest that what made the Garden of Eden so special wasn't the absence of work. It was the presence of the perfect co-worker. You see, I believe before things took a turn, God and his created beings worked *together*.

What if the perfect vision of work is not that we can be free of it entirely, but that we can be united in purpose, passion, and pursuit with God? What if we were called to work not out of punishment or duty, but in entrepreneurial partnership as part of God's original design?

Some may object to this idea, but actually in Genesis 2:5, the Hebrew word used for work is *abad* (or a*vad*), which means to work, serve, and even worship. God made us to work for Him and He wants to work *with* us. He wants us to create like Him and with Him. He wants to start, share, and complete new projects and ideas with us. He didn't leave Adam alone to tend to the Garden of Eden, and He doesn't ask us to work in isolation. Interestingly, God placed Adam in the garden to work it and take care of it, but the Bible doesn't say that God actually commanded him to do so. To work and keep it was simply part of the DNA of being human, of our function and purpose in the universe. God commanded Adam to eat from any tree in the garden except the tree of the knowledge of good and evil, but the command to work wasn't even necessary.

God uses us to bring about His kingdom on Earth as it is in heaven. As entrepreneurs, we get to take the potential of the earth and creatively make it better. With our Inspirer, our creations can bring order out of chaos, solve problems, seize opportunities, rally against injustice, and create dignity and opportunity for those who interact with our creations. How exactly we will do that, whatever our given focus and vision, is all about what we set up as the *structure* that will support the order of the business we conduct.

God has given us this blueprint to model, almost like a map. In creating the map of our life it's important to know two things. It's important to know where we want to go/be (vision), but the only way I can draw a map to get there is to know where

I am currently. Which is why it is crucial for us to be honest with ourselves and check our "vital signs" every now and then.

So, take a moment to check your vital signs:

- Financial: *Are you bringing in money and being a good steward?*
- Spiritual: *Are you connected to God and His Word?*
- Emotional: *Do you have a handle on the emotions you feel during the day?*
- Relationship: *Are you aligned with the right people and how do you treat those people?*
- Mental: *Are you overwhelmed or have you created a system to accomplish tasks and bring you closer to your vision?*
- Physical: *How well are you taking care of your body?*

Once you know where you are right now, you can create a structure to improve the areas that are lacking. If your vision is clear, and you have the atmosphere needed to cultivate greatness, the next step is to set up the systems to carry out your vision.

CREATING STRUCTURE

On the third day, God continued to work off the atmosphere He created on day two. At this stage, the whole earth was still completely covered by water. If you had been there, you would have seen nothing but ocean, no land of any sort. Did you know that according to the U.S. Geological Survey (USGS.gov), if you leveled out the earth's surface today, you'd see there's enough water in the oceans to cover the entire planet to a depth of almost two miles?

Picture God commanding the dry land to appear. Parts of the ocean floor began rising up out of the water and kept on going until rolling hills were formed in some places, as well as great stretches of land in other places. At the same time, other parts of the ocean floor sank down to form underwater valleys and basins, so that the water drained off the land and into one place.

A big point on this I always want to remind you of is God did all this by the mighty power of His Word. Did you know that seashells have been found near the top of Mt Everest? It was once low enough to be under the sea![7]

---

[7] *www.montana.edu/everest/facts/summit-limestone.html*

On Day Three, God spoke again and commanded the land to produce all kinds of plants. If you had been there, you would have seen green grass, tall palm trees, and other vegetation spring up from the ground. God made the first plants all fully grown, but each kind with its own particular seed. This was so they would reproduce themselves and not something else. Grape vines did not change into mango trees, and peanuts did not change into coconuts.

Earth was now a very beautiful place. God had a good look at all that He had made. He was pleased with what He saw, and He declared it to be good.

Notice that Day Two is the only day in which God does not expressly say of His work, "It was good" (Gen.1:4, 10, 12, 18, 21, 25). It cannot mean that the second day's work was not good. But it does seem to imply that the work of Day Two was an incomplete step toward making the earth habitable. He created the atmosphere but it was incomplete because no living creature could live yet. You can have an atmosphere that destroys or one that produces life.

The stage of creation that began on Day Two wasn't complete until Day Three, when dry land emerged from the water and the earth was made fit for living things. At that point, the world was finally shaped into a habitable condition, and then God pronounced His verdict: "It was good" (v. 10).

In business, like in marriage, it's important to have a plan and meet regularly to discuss this plan. If you've established an atmosphere of open acceptance and grace, that's good, now you can create a good business plan. If the atmosphere is bad, it's inevitable you will create a bad business plan. That's why it is so important to follow the process that God set out in His seven-day model.

What's your company structure? What's your product or service? Have you done any market research or analysis on where to plant those seeds (marketing) to reproduce "according to its kind?"

From there I like to take it a next step to a business playbook which basically lists all of your company's processes, policies, and standard operating procedures (SOPs) in one place. It also outlines exactly how your business does what it does, down to each role, responsibility, business strategy, and differentiator. It leaves nothing to guess. *[note: for more on creating this, see the resources on my website: RyleeMeek.com]*

Regardless of size or industry, every business needs a business playbook to run smoothly and scale successfully. It should be filled with all your documented processes, policies, and procedures. After all, championship sports teams win because they have the right players and a solid playbook. Scaling your business is no different! You can't scale a company with one or two superstars. Business is a team effort.

Yes, you need a roster filled with top talent. But you also need all your top plays documented, so your processes and policies exist outside your head and anyone can run them. That way, what your business does is scalable beyond just you. Most importantly, it can run without you!

I remember when I was trying to get my daughter Ellie to get into sports. We had her try out for soccer. She was more concerned about the butterflies and not getting kicked than she was about the ultimate goal, to score a goal. They didn't have a playbook, which ended up with having everyone running after the ball and crashing into each other. Not that it was vital to win at this young level, but this is forever a mental picture for me of "trying to win" vs. having a gameplan to win. Not to mention, most of the kids had no interest in being there (atmosphere), let alone a desire to win (vision).

Imagine you're out sick this week and none of your responsibilities are documented (or your team doesn't know where that documentation is). That means your responsibilities don't happen. Or, it means the rest of your team guesses how they do things, and they'll likely make a mistake. While making a mistake on, say, a social post might not be a big deal, a mistake in payroll could be.

This is the importance of having a clear structure in place, for anything you are looking to create and grow. Without it, you can't be as effective or responsive to normal fluctuations.

Now, the last thing about Day Three I like to point out is this: just like God created land first and then vegetation, and each with its own seed "according to its kind," we can think about the product or service we're offering as our specific seeds. This will be useful when we get to Day Four to determine the trackable and measurable items we can implement to establish order.

By creating a workable structure, we get our gameplan, the playbook we want to implement, and that sets us up for developing the proper *order*, which we'll cover next in Day Four. Having all of this in place is what will get us to the next phase of momentum and multiplication, and the results of the specific "seeds" we're looking to replicate.

CHAPTER FIVE

DAY FOUR
DETERMINING YOUR ORDER

And God said, "Let there be lights in the expanse of the heavens to separate the day from the night. And let them be for signs and for seasons, and for days and years, and let them be lights in the expanse of the heavens to give light upon the earth." And it was so. And God made the two great lights—the greater light to rule the day and the lesser light to rule the night—and the stars. ...And God saw that it was good. And there was evening and there was morning, the fourth day. (Genesis 1:14-19)

But all things must be done properly and in an orderly way. (1 Corinthians 14:40)

> **Main Takeaway:** *Establishing the proper order for your business operations ensures you can scale and respond to needs effectively to sustain momentum in the next phase.*

The fourth day's activity confuses some as God created the sun, moon, and stars after he created light. Our human tendency is to see the sun, moon, and stars as the source of light, but as mentioned in Day One (vision), God is light. These three sources of light are under God's rule. As it is written, the lights God created were set to rule the day and the night, the days and years, and the seasons. These lights that God created to rule over time and seasons are set to endure as long as the earth remains. Once again, God saw what he had created was good, and I believe it wasn't just in the physical qualities of these amazing heavenly bodies, but in the ordering and structuring of time He'd made possible through them.

SUCCESS IS ALL ABOUT THE PROCESS

Although we can summarize a good, basic business model in three steps, this isn't just about the second step in 1) Creating Vision (Purpose), 2) Developing Strategy (Process), and 3) Measuring Impact (Proof). We need to appreciate more fully the power of carefully ordering our business processes.

As a Kingdom Entrepreneur, much of what sets us apart from others in the marketplace is not so much *what* we're offering or selling (though sometimes it is), it's *how* we're conducting our business. The way we structure and then order or arrange our work should be a bit different than the status quo.

I've often taught that a great part of what distinguishes us from secular entrepreneurs is we know *why* we are called to create. We believe God has created us to share in His entrepreneurial process. We also know our identity is in Christ: we live lives that have been transformed by the Gospel, having accepted the gift of salvation, and now we seek to bring God glory as our highest purpose.

Another difference we have as Christians is that we steward creation rather than own it, acknowledging that God owns everything. We understand that He has entrusted these resources to us to steward effectively according to His purposes rather than our own. We do not worship work, but worship *with* our work. We're not to make work an idol that steals our affections from God and robs us of time for community, family, and fitness. But we believe excellence matters, so we should follow the example of our Savior and seek excellence in every aspect of our daily life, and strive to be willing versus willful, seeking to submit our will to God's, rather than mistake our will for His.

Before we move to discussing how to order our business, we should talk a little about this last point. Because that's the trick. An entrepreneur needs to be on guard about being willful vs. willing. Chip Ingram describes the paradigm as "striving vs. contending."[8] In essence, all of God's work is going to be done in a hostile environment where the enemy seeks to thwart Kingdom advancement. Therefore, it requires energy and focus and faith to move forward. But there's a difference between "contending" for the faith (what God has directed you to do), and "striving." Contending means "I bring all that I am in obedience to the Lord Jesus but the outcomes are His". It's a position of dependency and entrusting the results, and timing, and funding to Him. "Striving" is characterized by an internal pressure that "I have to make this happen" in my energy, in the timeline I believe is necessary and, in many cases, by the means that I think is best.

Basically, contending is accompanied by peace and dependency; striving is accompanied by anxiety and pressure.

I like to say the way we implement proper order in business is by thinking of this as *having goals with a deadline.*

---

[8] Faith Driven Entrepreneur, Henry Kaestner, J. D. Greear, Chip Ingram, Tyndale Ill., 2021.

When you want to establish the daily disciplines, routines, and action-triggers within your business structure you've created, these are your first steps that get you to the next day of creation having to do with momentum.

Don't get hung up on applying all of this just yet. If you've thought through your *why,* now's the time to think a bit about the *how.* It's often the case that ambitious people get caught up in being perfect when what's needed is to simply get some things done. I know from experience that rushing forward also encourages plagues of personal attitude (worry, doubt, fear, indecision, imposter syndrome, etc.) to appear. *Unlearning* bad habits and letting go of the shadows of past failures can help you go further than learning a new strategy on how to do something. For example, you could learn how to run faster by diving into the science of running, or you can first take off the 40-pound backpack you have been carrying around for years.

GOD'S ESTABLISHING OF ORDER

Consider how on Day Four of creation, God created the "ordering" of heavenly bodies—the sun, moon and stars—and declared them "good," as sources of light, and as ways to mark the passage of time. And "while the earth remains, seedtime and harvest, cold and heat, summer and winter, day and night, shall not cease" (Genesis 8:22), it'd be easy to take this for granted, as though He just pointed and *poof!* there was the sun. Who knows how this actually took place, but whatever did happen, can we even imagine how incredible God is?

Our solar system is well thought-out, my friends. Earth is about 93 million miles away from the sun, exactly the right distance to hold the temperature between 0°C and 40°C on most of the earth, the temperature needed to sustain most life. If we were just 5% closer to the sun, the oceans would boil and the water would all evaporate. If the earth was only 5% further away, the oceans would freeze.

Also, if Earth's speed of rotation about its own axis were any slower than it is, our days would be unbearably hot and our nights freezing cold. If the rotation were much faster, the wind would blow so strongly that you wouldn't be able to stand up in the open. The length of each day and night is also just right for the amount of sleep we need.

The pull of gravity on the earth by the moon and the sun causes the tides which cleanse the ocean's shores, help put oxygen (that fish breathe) into the water, and help keep the ocean currents moving, preventing the sea from becoming stagnant. The huge planet, Jupiter, with its strong gravity, is in just the right position to pull many comets and meteors away from crashing into Earth and killing us all.

I could go on and on, but God certainly knew what He was doing. The Bible says that His eternal power and divine nature can be seen from the things He has made (Romans 1:20). Seasons of time are possible because of Day Four, which I believe we need to appreciate in order to run a successful business. A good product and a target market is good, but it isn't enough, at some point you'll want to take your business to the next level. A lot of entrepreneurs fail at this step, but it's crucial for establishing your process and creating momentum that will ultimately scale as you begin to multiply in days five and six.

ORDERING YOUR BUSINESS

Just starting is one of the most difficult "seasons" in any business, and it's important to remember that little saying that "you cannot manage what you don't measure." God has given us the gift of time and the ability to track and measure things in order to manage them. In business, tracking and analyzing your metrics is critical to long-term success. What are business metrics? Simply put, they're the numbers showing you the vital data about your business processes. By regularly tracking and assessing the metrics, you can determine if your efforts are moving you towards success or failure.

In general, there are two types of business metrics: operational and financial. Operational metrics are related to the performance of your employees, as well as the overall efficiency of your business. They could be related to your turnaround time, production time, or the time it takes to respond to customer's queries.

Most teams work from a computer these days, so tracking performance levels could involve tracking employee computer activity. You can easily do this with a simple employee computer monitoring software which doesn't have to be intrusive at all. The best computer system monitoring software on the market will act as a project tracking software as well, so you'll be able to check how much time your employees needed to finish every task within the project, and it will be easy to determine project profitability as well.

The other metric to track is financial. Financial metrics include your profitability ratios, ROIs on marketing campaigns, sales figures, etc. You can track financial metrics by using billing and payment software. By doing so you'll have all your incoming and outgoing payments in one place. Pair this up with a time tracking tool, and you've got yourself a winner. Especially if you're billing clients and paying employees by the hour.

WHY BOTHER?

Again, you can't manage what you don't measure. Tracking the right business metrics is vital to improving company performance. With so many possible business metrics, it's important to choose the ones that matter most to your business.

Every business should track its performance in sales, marketing, finance and human resources (HR) in order to know how it is doing and how it might improve performance. In order for you to make decisions, you need to rely on data. Metrics, as well as decisions based on them, are used for improvement. Additionally, they can help you shift your focus to your most important assets.

You should use them as grounds for new financial and marketing strategies, as well as for improving relationships with your customers, distributors and employees. Proper metrics should be giving you answers to the following questions:

What were your results in the past?

What are your goals for the future?

Is there something that should be improved?

Which targets did you reach?

Which targets did you miss?

Once you have this data, it's important to note that you communicate these metrics and targets to your team clearly. It will be much easier for your team to shift their behavior, and make changes during the working process so they can reach the goal. It isn't very practical when you say "We need more sales" or "We need to reduce the number of complaints." However, when you say "We need to reduce the number of complaints by 20% by the end of the quarter," your employees know exactly what you mean and that there's a measurable goal for achieving this.

This is all part of the ordering of business, and we'll really begin to see how important order is when we get to Day Five, "Momentum."

PART III

DEPLOY

"Now that you know these things, you will be blessed if you do them." – John 13:17

"For the provision of God constantly to be at work in our lives we must activate the laws of God." – Phil Pringle

Part III, *Deploy*, is ensuring you make the most of every opportunity to hit the market strong, obtain your goals, and ultimately create the momentum and sustained growth you desire as you apply the final steps of the 7-day system.

CHAPTER SIX

DAY FIVE
GAINING MOMENTUM

And God said, "Let the waters swarm with swarms of living creatures, and let birds fly above the earth across the expanse of the heavens." So God created the great sea creatures and every living creature that moves, with which the waters swarm, according to their kinds, and every winged bird according to its kind. And God saw that it was good. And God blessed them, saying, "Be fruitful and multiply and fill the waters in the seas, and let birds multiply on the earth." And there was evening and there was morning, the fifth day. (Genesis 1:20-23)

"Now may the God of peace, who brought up from the dead the great Shepherd of the sheep through the blood of the eternal covenant, that is, Jesus our Lord, equip you in every good thing to do His will, working in us that which is pleasing in His sight, through Jesus Christ, to whom be the glory forever and ever. Amen. (Hebrews 13:21, NASB)

> **Main Takeaway:** *Since all your preparations come to fruition in the activation of momentum, evaluating the effectiveness of your business's movement and operations is essential.*

Now we've seen why it's important to have all these things in place for your business to operate effectively—vision, atmosphere, structure, and order. But without the element of momentum added in Day Five, it would all be for naught.

On the fifth day of creation, God created more life. Once again, he sees it as good. But this time he adds something else:

> *"And God blessed them, saying, "Be fruitful and multiply and fill the waters in the seas, and let birds multiply on the earth"* (Genesis 1:22).

The blessing of the Lord enters the world on Day Five. He creates every living thing that moves, but then he also ensures his living creatures will continue and proliferate by giving them the ability through a blessing to be fruitful and multiply. This big addition to His process is what the third and final part of our big business plan rests on—*"Deploy"*—this essential ability that comes in the form of God's blessing to multiply.

I believe recognizing this pronouncement as a gift is one of our great business advantages. When I was just starting out, I had that common dissatisfaction so many have, knowing I wanted to make a bigger contribution and do something great for the Kingdom. I just didn't know what. I had to learn to listen to that voice, and then to try different things, like rough drafts of business visions and plans. And it wasn't until failing multiple times at various things that I realized that strong voice of dissatisfaction was there because I had some important inner work to do. In fact, working out this plan for business success based on the seven days of creation is part of that bigger work and the result of God's heavy work in me.

I don't live in regret and you know I'm a firm believer in seeking the positive. But I've had my share of disappointments and it's always interesting to look back and see where I was missing some vital preparation or life knowledge that could have enhanced and refined my vision. All of us struggle with what we lack, but I know once we come to learn what's missing and we gain those things or needed insights, we appreciate them all the more for the difficulty we faced.

I'd been selling a variety of things for many years before I hit a low point in 2011 and was essentially homeless for a while, sleeping on my sister's couch. Coming off a failed business venture, I was broke and had no idea what I was going to do next. I knew I could get a job or start selling something again, but I didn't want to work for somebody else anymore.

I spent many late nights searching the Internet trying to figure out what the heck I was going to do next. One night, I was online searching, looking for new business ventures, marketing ideas, whatever I could find, and I came across an ad on Craigslist. It said "Work three days a week, make $10,000." That sounded pretty good, but of course, I thought, *Yeah, right!*

Still, I was curious, so I decided to figure out what this was. I called the number and talked with the guy back and forth a few times. He said he did this seminar selling to groups of people, and it didn't really hit me what he was referring to until I drove down about an hour and a half to sit in on one of these presentations. I walked into the room and it completely blew my mind. There were 24 people sitting there. The guy delivered a presentation, and at the end he simply asked for an appointment to have people meet with him the next day. He got seven appointments, and it completely rocked my world. I thought, *Man, if this guy could do one presentation a week, and only meet with the people that wanted to know more? Holy cow! This is it!*

That was the beginning of Social Dynamic selling. It would take me a few years to really understand how to do it (which I describe more fully in my book, *Food For Thought)*, but that started me on the trail toward what I'd end up doing for the next 10 years and generating momentum.

THE VALUE OF VISION

We covered this on Day One, but I want to highlight its importance. Life is a dance. It has a rhythm. Seasons, months, weeks, and days all have a rhythm and an order to them, and we do best to observe the way they flow and how they organize our lives. I often tell clients to go back to their vision and think about that first emotional connection they had to it, to find the "why" for their life and work. Knowing this ensures they'll be able to get back on track when the storms and challenges come—and they will come, I assure you. I firmly believe there is no failure, just feedback, but nothing I've gotten has come easy. Nothing worth having, anyway.

The difference between motivation and inspiration is that motivation continually requires new outside sources, while inspiration comes from a deeper inner source. This inspiration fuels our vision and the determination for progress, momentum. I believe this deeper source of inspiration is what we need to appreciate most about God's blessing in Day Five.

Reminding yourself of this source of your vision gives purpose to the struggle of carrying it out. Like Friedrich Nietzsche once said, "He who has a why to live can bear almost any how." It's important to stay connected to your vision so you stay the course you set for yourself, knowing that distractions and temporary things are nothing compared to what you've committed to. It will be worth it in the end. Like in the movie *Rocky*, during the extra tough workouts to train and get himself in shape, Rocky constantly reminds himself of his *why* (which is making a better life for Adrian, the love of his life) and that pushes him through the hard times. Another word for this is called *anchoring*, where you anchor yourself to your deep, emotional reason to keep moving forward. It's very effective and I've used it so many times. For me, it's my wife Ash and my daughter Ellie.

Our knowledge comes from our past experience, and our mood comes from our future, what we see taking shape and believe we're moving toward with determination and hard work. If you keep your focus on what will be achieved in the future, you will keep moving towards it. I believe this is what God demonstrated in the first few days of creation when He set up the world and the ecosystem for what He knew was coming in Day Five.

THE CREATION OF MOMENTUM

Everything God had created up until now was setting the stage for this day. He needed to create water, air, land, plants, and trees first to sustain what he was planning. This is why I like to focus on Day Five as the culmination or the result of everything else that came before. On Day Five, I believe God created not just animals but he also created what we can now see as *movement* or the momentum of his creation plan. It wasn't just for some pretty water, rocks, and sky. It wasn't just a sun and a moon and stars to look good and create the proper atmosphere. The aquatic animals and flying creatures were created to live in the spaces God had prepared for them previously. Now we see why He did what He did on the previous days. Everything was prepared for what He had planned for this day, the big implementation of His master plan to sustain and bless these self-sustaining, living, breathing creatures.

Think about how intricately God thought through the cycle of life for all these creatures depending on each other for survival. He made flying animals to pollinate the world's plants and food crops, crops that would be used for biofuels, fibers, craft and construction materials, medicine, and livestock feed. He made seabirds to eat fish, crustaceans, and their guano (droppings) where they nest to fertilize plants and even coral reefs. The ecosystem is beyond incredible. Fish contribute essential nutrients that support their ecosystem as well, recycling the nutrients that algae and other species need to survive so they in turn can support other creatures.

Or think how we've learned from fish and birds how forming schools and flocks helps protect against predators, improve foraging, and nest more efficiently. These communities are examples for all of us to learn to work within and benefit from the power and camaraderie of groups. And this is just the tip of the iceberg of all God demonstrated in ordering his creation of the world the way He did. The point of all of this is that *the setup is more important than we tend to think.* When we plan for the fulfillment of our vision, create the proper atmosphere and culture, and think through the structure and the order of operations first, then we can know we're ready to truly begin and sustain momentum for the long haul of actually earning a profit and creating movement in doing business.

God didn't just create all life with the ability to perpetuate their species by reproduction and say, "Go to it." He designed the way in which all He made would operate and interact, and this great care is what made the work so *good.*

WHAT'S YOUR PLAN?

All that time I was broke and looking for the next thing, the fulfilling work we do now became the fuel for my momentum when I started Social Dynamic Selling. Seeing how effective it was convinced me to get invested, but I didn't have a clue what my plan should be or how I was going to get from A to B, let alone get rich. But I knew enough about this guy's model to know I just needed to send out some postcards and invite people to a presentation so I could make some sales. Slowly but surely, I kept reinvesting into growing that business. It was just the bare bones of a plan, but it worked because now I could leverage my time, marketing, and the energy and effort I was spending in one-on-one sales into one dinner seminar.

This is the beauty of what happened in Day Five. God took the structure and order He'd previously designed and then employed it to sustain life. The idea was embedded in the original vision, though it only existed in His mind at that point. God's "business plan" for life on Earth was designed for everything to work together for the good of each other. But He had to imagine how all the activity would need to operate and function *before* it happened so it could run smoothly once everything to support it was in place when the time came.

Many people are held back in business because of a lack of the preparations that are needed first. When I was just starting out, I took that trip trip to Kuala Lumpur, Malaysia, in an effort to get established there. I had no vision, no long-term prospects for ongoing sales, and no sense of what I wanted my business to look like in a month, let alone several months or years out. I didn't properly prepare. I didn't know what I didn't know. I only knew what I didn't want, which was to end up around the wrong people with no life direction. This is how people get into trouble. I wound up flying right home, and I learned an important lesson about business: have a plan.

It would take many years before I'd eventually learn how to set my own course for success, to have a vision, plan a structure, and think through the order of needed activity to gain momentum and multiplication. But when the life of your business begins, too many people simply launch into selling and expect instant success. The whole goal of this book is to help you put first things first. You need to develop a clearly communicated vision based in what you want to see happen, whatever you see your day-to-day activity being. So, you set that vision first, imagining what's needed to create the proper atmosphere and culture for your work to thrive, and then you need to **implement** what the structure will need to be to support that vision, and then comes the order of when to do the various things required within that support structure, based on who's responsible for what.

Only then are you ready to begin; once you've created all that's needed to support the product or service, the purpose, movement, and momentum of the business. In any partnership, if you're assisting each other and taking into account each other's duties and responsibilities, and operating in excellence, doing your job so the other can do theirs, then you can gain momentum. In business, when we have a clear vision, the atmosphere is good, we have a business plan and playbook, and we're handling our responsibilities, then our Day Five is when we can start the machine and begin to gain momentum. When the marketing is producing leads, the sales team is selling, and the fulfillment team is taking care of the new customers, the company will begin to work. That's when you're set up for momentum and increase.

This is the goal! When we are all working for the purpose of being fruitful and multiplying, there is no small role. In fact, when you're operating with other believers you can see this as the beginning stages of a new body of Christ working together, a perfectly orchestrated creation!

Once we have this dialed in, then and only then can we move on to the exciting Day Six, *Multiply.*

CHAPTER SEVEN

DAY SIX
BEGINNING TO MULTIPLY

And God said, "Let the earth produce living creatures according to their kind…" and it was so. …and God saw that it was good. Then God said, "Let Us make mankind in Our image, according to Our likeness…" So God created man in His own image… God blessed them; and God said to them, "Be fruitful and multiply, and fill the earth, and subdue it…" And it was so. And God saw all that He had made, and behold, it was very good. And there was evening and there was morning, the sixth day. (Genesis 1:24, 26-28, 31)

"Bad company corrupts good character." (1 Corinthians 15:33, NKJV)

> **Main Takeaway:** *Relationships are the capstone, the pinnacle of creation, and as such, we represent our Maker in the quality and effectiveness of our business partnerships.*

On the sixth day of creation, God created mankind, but He also created the first human relationship so we could multiply and take dominion. When you consider it, things escalated pretty quickly on this day. God created all the different kinds of animals and "everything that creeps on the ground" and sees them as good, and then He says, *"Let Us make mankind in Our image,"* giving an early nod to the Trinity of Father (Creator), Son (Redeemer) and Holy Spirit (Guide). There's a lot more to this than first meets the eye, but importantly, on this day God created connected *relationships*.

It wasn't merely between man and woman either. It was between God and man and them and the animals, plants, and earth, and all of it was blessed and overseen and designed by God's careful creative work. The plan was complete at the end of the sixth day. The entire universe in all its beauty and perfection, fully formed, and all His work completed, God announces that it is "very good." I believe we can draw some conclusions about why He emphasizes this as He looks out on everything He has made and sees what it represents. Specifically for our discussion, I think there's a lot to appreciate about these relationships between all these things, and as we will see, it's this unique interaction of back-and-forth partnership that I think best reveals the reason for His joy.

WHY RELATIONSHIPS MATTER MOST

Many of us place a high priority on our relationships, whether or not we remember to respect them or even treat everyone fairly all the time. Often, our outer responses and actions don't match our inner beliefs. But most of us would at least say we agree that relationships in life are very important, maybe even what life is all about. I'd certainly say that at this point, and in some way, even based on my early decisions, I can see I've always sensed there's something vitally important in being connected and committed to the people who are most important to us in life.

I honestly think one very early memory of mine is the start of my marketing and sales career. I grew up in a small town in South Dakota with less than 1,000 people, and my folks got divorced when I was five years old. I'm the youngest of three, and when I look back, I see I was a people pleaser and I didn't know this then, but I always wanted to keep the peace. When I was with my dad, I would literally sneak away and hide under the bed with the corded phone and call my mom to tell her how much I missed her and wanted to be with her. And then at my mom's, I would hide in the closet and try to call my dad. I was playing both sides. I missed them, and time always feels like an eternity when you're that young, but mainly I didn't want the other parent to think I loved one more than the other. I felt this constant turmoil, and I made that vow many kids of divorce make, that I would never put my child through what I went through. Which, of course, set me up for another big failure. But more on that later.

We often hear how sales is all about relational management and trust, and that's true, but I think it's important to really think about why that is. The King's Council is based on relationship and alignment, specifically our relationship with God and our alignment with His purpose. That is our primary consideration, based on the greatest commandment Jesus gives in Matthew 22:37, to "love the Lord your God with all your heart and with all your soul and with all your mind." But we also affirm the second greatest commandment as an extension of the first, to "love your neighbor as yourself" (v. 39). Not only is this how to keep the original commandments and the teaching of the prophets, but it's also how we can build lives and businesses of integrity, vision, and purpose, through powerful relationships.

There's this great agreement in the Bible between Genesis and the prophets and the gospels and Paul's letters. Even beyond Jesus' original teaching, remember to continue always searching for the three kinds of personal relationships we all need, a Paul to learn from, a Barnabas to lean on, and a Timothy to mentor. Stay open to everyone and work to show love, even when you find some irreconcilable differences with someone, to learn from them. Keeping your vision focused on what you know God's calling to be *for you* is essential, as well as keeping the first commandment to love God first, and others second.

I believe it's this commitment—to knowing who God has called us to be and honoring our personality and experiences that made us who we are—that allows us to properly emphasize relationships and figure out who we most need to be around. We all face times of disagreement and struggle when we'll have to draw on our wisdom and character to discern what seems best. We may not know what to do in new circumstances, but if we stay committed to God and these two commandments, and remember them as our deepest purposes, our lives and businesses will be able to withstand the challenges and even flourish in adversity. There's no guarantee of this, of course, but we can know we've remained faithful and true to what God has called us to by applying one simple rule Jesus encouraged us to apply: *look for the fruit.*

HOW TO FIND GOOD BUSINESS PARTNERS

"For no good tree bears bad fruit, nor again does a bad tree bear good fruit, for each tree is known by its own fruit" (Luke 6:43-44).

This simple idea has saved me so many times when I've been unsure about what do to in any given relationship. It's a philosophy I've become so committed to in life and business, simply looking for the fruit. I've figured out which path to take and who to glean from by looking at what someone's life is producing and comparing that against what they claim. Not in a judgmental way or to call people out, unless God specifically asks me to, but just looking at the people's lives you want to emulate, and who you want to be around. It's important to be around them and see what you could learn about how they live. When you do that, you'll see. Someone may have a great Instagram persona, but is there fruit? This isn't stuff you typically hear in many business books but I think it has to be a big part of the total package.

Because of this, I've had to learn to take a more intentional approach to my business relationships. It's important to get insight and be careful to include tons of grace with people because we're no better than anyone, and much of the time I don't actually know what they're dealing with. We should only ask questions without judgment and remember "a gentle answer turns away wrath" (Proverbs 15:1, NASB).

But if you're committed to this, to excellence and true partnership, transparency is vital, so plan to help them if they're struggling. You might even have ideas of ways you could help ease the pressure on them. And remember, if you're going to help people be more excellent mentally, emotionally, physically, spiritually, and financially, you'd better be operating in this manner yourself. You have to have fruit in your life that people want, and it's so often the case that when you get to know someone, they're not who you thought they were, but if they get around the right people, maybe they could be one day. If they're not willing to hear hard truths with grace, maybe it's time to part ways.

Relating well is hard because it's difficult to integrate all the pieces of who we truly are, and it's work for all of us.

That's why my firm belief now is that if you're going to go into business with somebody, you have to date them first. You've got to understand and see what they're like at home, what their family life is like, and even in little things that show how they live. You need to go be with them before you get into business with them.

My business relationships and partnerships have taught me more than anything else about effective Kingdom management, and through these men and women, the good and the difficult, I know God has worked a complete transformation in me. As we become closer with God and others, all our relationships benefit, and there's always so much more to learn. But He will show you where you need to go if you pay attention and do your part to support and value the good in people.

Bottom line, I believe this is how we can best exercise dominion in the business world, by emphasizing the value of relationships. That doesn't mean we will click and jive with everyone, but we must use this idea of taking dominion as God's blessing to claim territory for Him by scaling our companies responsibly and appropriately, and working to increase God's Kingdom of love here on earth. Once you have a solid vision, a sustainable culture, systems in place, and you've properly ordered things, momentum has begun, and soon it will be time to multiply that success by adding some strategic relationships.

AN ENTREPRENEUR'S RELATIONSHIPS

One of the greatest times in my life was when I was in college at Normandale Community College in Bloomington, MN. I had such a great tribe of brothers. We would spend late nights studying the bible, worshipping, even hitting the streets of Minneapolis to witness to folks. It was truly an amazing experience for me. Some of the most incredible bonds were formed. To this day, I feel like I could call any of those guys and if I needed a body moved, they would ask, "Are you driving or am I?" We've since gone on in our lives, but that's been my picture of what community is ever since. A true brotherhood.

We all know there's family of origin and family of choice. Your family of origin—parents, grandparents, step-families and in-laws—won't always be as close as your family of choice, those you choose to connect with. Observing Ecclesiastes 4:9, which says, "Two are better than one because they have a good return for their labor" (NASB), we have to take time to consider who best aligns with your vision and goals. Whether it's your marriage, your parenting, your business, your friendships, or your business alignments, there is value in knowing the vision for that relationship, and all parties need to contribute their part and have clear expectations.

If we can share our hopes and fears with each other and commit to our roles and respective tasks, God can bless our work by multiplying it. When we look closely at how God set about creating the land animals, He created them each "according to their kind" (Genesis 1:24). What were these "kinds"? Moses records the animals in three broad categories: livestock, such as sheep, goats, and cattle; creeping things, such as insects, worms, and reptiles; and the wild animals, like lions, foxes, and kangaroos. Man has distinct responsibilities and relationships with each of these kinds, and like with the different kinds of plants, part of the work is figuring out which kinds are most useful for his work. There's an underlying message of the circle of life here.

Day Six is all about responsibility and stewardship. Just think about all the relationships that begin on Day Six. God places the first man in a garden to care for it (Genesis 2:15), and says, "It is not good for the man to be alone. I will make a helper suitable for him" (verse 18, NASB). God makes a woman to be with him (vs. 21–22) and then places them in authority over the earth and over all the other creatures (v. 26). God blesses them and says to multiply, fill the earth, and "subdue" it—that is, steward it (v. 28). After declaring it "very good," humanity is given the decree, which is also our Kingdom Entrepreneur mandate: be fruitful (productive) and multiply (reproduce); fill the earth (distribute) and subdue it (master the market).

Making us "in His own image" means we reflect God in our ability to love (1 John 4:19), to reason (Isaiah 1:18), and to make intelligent decisions (Deuteronomy 30:19). Mankind is uniquely and intimately formed by God (Isaiah 45:12). In this original perfection, God also gives the first humans a moral responsibility, to use their free will and capacity to decide morally, to not eat of one tree. With the authority to rule comes the responsibility to rule well. There is an inherent accountability in the command to subdue the earth. Man has a duty to exercise his dominion under the authority of the One who delegated it, since all true authority is from God (Romans 13:1-5). Man is to bring the material world and all its various parts into the service of God for the good of mankind. The command to subdue the earth is actually part of God's blessing on mankind.

So, we are to have dominion, but what does that actually mean?

UNDERSTANDING "DOMINION"

I think it's helpful to think of it this way: As God's image bearers in creation, we were intended to act as His representatives. We were designed, in a very real way, to show the world what God is like. When God gave us the command to rule over the earth, the expectation was to do so in a way that reflected His character.

If you were to ask someone to watch your kids, you wouldn't just say, "Do whatever you want." You would expect the babysitter to maintain the rules the family has in place. The babysitter is to act as a representative (albeit in an extremely limited sense) of you and your spouse. Human dominion is a little like that, but on a much grander scale. When God placed the first man in the garden of Eden, it was to "work it and keep it" (Genesis 2:15). Adam was commanded to take care of the earth, to fill and cultivate the rest of it following after the example God had given him in the garden.

This was the ideal—and yet, as we can see just looking out our windows, it's clear we're not living in a paradise. There are some wondrous things in our world, no question, but let's be honest, it's a mess. In the beginning, the ground yielded its fruit gladly to the man; work wasn't toil. But when man sinned, God put him under a curse and everything, including the earth, was affected. So rather than yielding fruit easily, the earth rebelled against the man, giving him thorns and thistles instead of the fruit of his labors.

Rather than using our dominion to cultivate the earth, we've chosen to conquer it instead. In a very real sense, this is the curse many folks still labor under. Thank God He sent Jesus to redeem us!

REDEEMING DOMINION IN A FALLEN WORLD

I don't believe dominion is simply about how we treat nature or the environment. It also involves how we interact with the world around us. This idea of proper, humble dominion touches every part of our being, and despite our fallen state, God has not removed the charge to rule over the earth. So, we must consider how to use the authority God has given us to bring Him glory.

Plain and simple: financial prosperity brings increased authority and responsibility in our world. It's true: more money, more problems. When I started making money with Social Dynamic, I didn't yet have the maturity I needed to steward it wisely. I required a couple years of counseling with great Christian mentors, and the love of my wife Ashley, as well as some amazing business partners and friends to help set me straight and speak truth into my life. From the very beginning of selling, hosting seminars, to going through the divorce I said I'd never get, and wanting to ensure my daughter would have everything she needed regardless of the mess I'd made, I still knew and believed God works things out for the good of those who love Him and commit to live according to His purpose.

I'm proof that the sovereignty of God is bigger than any false notion of my life or vision I ever had. My journey has proven to me over and over that I'm called to take dominion and pursue this specific purpose for His glory and to further His Kingdom. So that's not something I can take lightly.

There are so many more principles we could unpack about the Kingdom economy and stewarding it, but much of that is yet to come on the podcast and in the training seminars and other books in this series. To close this last big idea out, here are three suggestions for what I think taking dominion looks like, loosely based on Genesis 1:28:

1. Steward creation responsibly. Take care of what you have been given. Appreciate it. Honor it.

2. Work with excellence. While few of us are in positions of great authority, we are all responsible for carrying out the work we've been given with excellence. Do your work well, respect your employers, remembering that "you are serving the Lord Christ," not men (Colossians 3:24).

3. Multiply spiritually. God's blessing gives us the ability to multiply in many good things—children obviously, but in many other ways as well. We can bring new life into the world in so many ways. And that's a big deal! We multiply spiritually when we are effective ambassadors of the love of Jesus Christ, sharing the news of Jesus' sin-defeating death and resurrection with the world. We are to make disciples of

all nations. I believe this is one of the greatest ways we can exercise dominion over the earth, by using the authority given by Christ for the express purpose of seeing the lost become found.

Some of the top businesses, the most successful people in the world, operate by these three principles, and you don't have to be a believer to have them work. But when you do see them working, and you know where they come from, you see why the Kingdom Economy is so powerful.

My goal here has been to make you aware of these principles and how you can be successful employing them too, so we can have more Christians in positions of authority and influence. As mentioned, I've seen some of the top businessmen in the world operating by these principles for decades, simply because they work. But when you're a believer and your heart is for the Kingdom, it's my firm belief that operating by these principles is how we can take some serious territory back for the Kingdom.

CHAPTER EIGHT

DAY SEVEN
KEEPING THE SABBATH

Thus the heavens and the earth were finished, and all the host of them. And on the seventh day God finished his work that he had done, and he rested on the seventh day from all his work that he had done. So God blessed the seventh day and made it holy, because on it God rested from all his work that he had done in creation. (Genesis 2:1-3)

Come to me, all who labor and are heavy laden, and I will give you rest. Take my yoke upon you, and learn from me, for I am gentle and lowly in heart, and you will find rest for your souls. For my yoke is easy, and my burden is light. (Matthew 11:28-30)

> **Main Takeaway:** *Weekly rest provides time and space to refine your operations, create staying power, and increase your business's effectiveness and productivity.*

After creating the heavens and the earth in six days, we all know what God did on the last day: He rested. But, he seventh day is considered a day of creation because God set it apart as special. Did God need rest? It's hard to imagine. More likely, He was demonstrating something important for us to understand.

The heavens and the earth were completed in all their vast array. But then God paused, took notice of what He created, and blessed all He had accomplished. In our go-all-the-time world, rest is often looked at as wasting time. However, rest is short for restoration, and we could all use more restoration in every part of our lives.

Your vision of your business must include adequate, even ample, time to rest. Once you put the system and an order of things together, you will need to reflect on what is and is not working. Relationships will need *review* to make sure they are in alignment with your vision.

The purpose of this seventh day of creation is to pause and take a look at all you are doing. Because there is always much to appreciate and evaluate in business.

One helpful question I've learned to ask on my day of rest is, *How can I duplicate myself best so I can better scale operations to the next level I envisioned?* I review the vision and the order of things, as well as the relationships. In relationships, the question is often, *How can I best serve others to help them leave space to bless God, their people, and this business?* Especially in today's world, effective businesses are led by leaders who understand the value and importance of rest for their partners, employees, and customers. Never stopping to rest, reflect, and review is like working hard to climb a ladder and then realizing at the top it's leaning against the wrong building. If you don't stop to rest, reflect, and review, you're going to end up pointed at the wrong goals.

Just as God decreed the entirety of his creation "very good" and then moved into his rest, this is a pattern to establish for all of us. God created the Sabbath so we could learn to honor His gifts and know why our heaven on earth includes both work and play.

THE DAY OF RENEWAL

God's rest denotes that His creation is complete. Likewise, our rest is a chance to evaluate what we've created, what's complete, and what's continuing next week. Further, God is establishing a pattern of one day in seven to rest. The keeping of this day will eventually be a distinguishing trait of God's chosen people, Israel (Exodus 20:8–11). God does not slumber or sleep (Psalm 121:4), but the Hebrew word here for rest also means "cease." God ceased His creative work after six days and we are meant to honor this pattern for our own health and benefit as well.

Taking at least a day to reflect on what we've completed can also be a way to recognize and consider the work God has done for us and with us, and how He takes care of us.

Consider God's blessing of this day and how Jesus says in Mark 2:27, "The Sabbath was made for man, not man for the Sabbath." Honoring this day is honoring the way we are made, to accept we need rest and renewal. Also consider how God only ceased new creative work on the seventh day, not all activity. If your work is physical, you may require extra recuperating, but just as God isn't distant from His creation, or leaving the universe to run by itself (John 5:17, Colossians 1:17, Hebrews 1:3), our day of rest might be active. We just may need a break from creating new things and making new plans.

God took six days to make everything to provide us this example of how to structure our week. Exodus 20:9-11 is the basis of the fourth commandment: "Six days you shall labor, and do all your work, but the seventh is a Sabbath to the Lord your God. On it you shall not do any work... For in six days the Lord made heaven and earth, the sea, and all that is in them, and rested on the seventh day." That is why a week is seven days long, not six days or eight. It is based on the way God made the universe during creation week.

Having a sabbath has not always factored into my operations. I always operated under the mentality that most entrepreneurs have: just work harder, grind, hustle. You can sleep when you're dead. It wasn't until recently that God revealed to me the importance of the Sabbath, at first out of necessity to recover from some very long weeks, and then eventually more intentionally, as I wanted to be more present to my family and friends. I've known plenty of entrepreneurs who didn't take a sabbath while starting out and as a result experienced burnout. I know there's pressure to perform perfectly and get a competitive advantage, and there will always be those times when it makes more sense just to get the jump on things or on the week by working through Sunday, even just a little. But I believe God honors those who honor His structure and order, and I'd rather be a day behind and give

Him the opportunity to surprise me with what He made happen without my help, than risk burning out and not honoring the way I'm made to rest. There are still times I forget and have to pay the price with fatigue or disappointing my family, but I'm continually training to up my sabbath game and incorporating rest into my full life.

I remember that the Sabbath and its keeping was a covenant between God and His people: ". . . this is a sign between me and you throughout your generations, that you may know that I, the Lord, sanctify you" (Exodus 31:13). God set aside this day for His people to find renewal as they sought His call and purpose. Who am I to mess with that? It's just easier to accept my human limits and let it be a reminder that God is in control, not me.

KEEPING IT HOLY

The nation of Israel was created to be an instrument through which God would bring salvation to the world. Because of this, the day of rest that helps lend structure to the week is vital to institute in any business operation. God called and re-calls us like He did the Israelites to a life sanctified through the keeping of a Sabbath.

It would be all too easy to assume this is a vestige of the past and we need to move on and get with the 21st Century. No one wants to be legalistic or religious about it, after all. I don't disagree. But like the Holy Spirit teaches, trains, and convicts us of sin so we can do what God has planned for us since the beginning, I believe taking a sabbath day is a chance for God to work in our absence. Is it a sin to work on Sunday? Many wise folks have believed so, but I like to think Paul is right in saying, "All things are permitted, but not all things are of benefit" (1 Corinthians 10:23, NASB). Maybe the question should be whether we're leaving enough space for the Spirit to convict us where we need it.

To this end, we pray, "Your kingdom come, your will be done, on earth as it is in heaven." (Matthew 6:10) That is not our own will, about work or rest or anything. Sanctified by the Sprit and the Word, as God's people, we are called to join Him in building His kingdom. It's this intentional rest that points to our identity as God's people, sanctified for His work.

God gave us this picture of intentional rest as a reminder of who we are, and to set us apart as His creation. It's not always our first thought, especially when there's much work to be done, but it's a blessing to us to live in this intended rhythm.

As a result, I've often found myself reflecting on a day off how grateful I am for it.

CHAPTER NINE

A FINAL WORD

So whether you eat or drink or whatever you do, do it all for the glory of God. (1 Corinthians 10:31)

As I said, there are many more ideas and principles to unpack about the Kingdom Economy. I plan to continue sharing more, and I look forward to connecting with many of you soon. I have a couple other parting thoughts to share about all this, and a bit of application. But first, let's quickly recap our 7-day method for Kingdom Entrepreneurship, just to ensure the basic process is clear:

1) Cast a *vision* to dispel darkness.

2) Create an *atmosphere* of a supportive, agreeable business culture.

3) Arrange the different tasks and needs of your business into an effective, clear *structure*.

4) Ensure the *order* of the processes of your business is complete and responsive to your needs.

5) Begin the movement of your operations and establish a rhythm to generate *momentum*.

6) Emphasize human relationships to *multiply* in good things and scale your business appropriately.

7) Include the blessing of *rest* on the seventh day to sanctify it and set an example.

Foundationally, these seven principles have formed my business operations and fueled my growth. I believe we can't be the most effective Kingdom Entrepreneurs without taking our time to invest in each of these considerations in sequence. And while these seven steps lay out the process of building effective, profitable businesses, they are based in four primary commitments I developed to help myself stay focused on what truly matters in life. These Kingdom principles apply to generating prosperity in business, which I believe we all need to understand:

Vision is about *ownership*–God owns everything in the Kingdom.

Money is about *stewardship*–Money is a tool expanding the Kingdom.

Tithing is a matter of *worship*—Positioning our hearts for blessing and being a blessing.

Our work and business are about *kinship*–Sowing & reaping together in God's world.

We haven't talked much about stewardship and tithing, but these are the subjects of my next two books. As a sneak peek, I hope to get you excited for the next installments of this Kingdom Entrepreneur training, and seeing a bit more of how this all fits together in our biblical model of effective business design, development, and deployment.

That last point could just as easily say it's about *"kingship,"* but "kinship" puts the focus on the "big why"— as believers, everything we do ultimately points to God, and for Him it's always for relationship.

I hope you've been able to appreciate how this 7-day model isn't so much a solution to plug in, as it is a simple way to think about all the elements you need to create a sustainable business over the long term. I like to think that with all biblical wisdom, it isn't a shortcut to apply but a *lifestyle* to enjoy.

In terms of what this all comes down to, all of this is about God, but it's also about others, which means everything we're doing and building and multiplying is ultimately serving the first and second commands to love God and others as ourselves. In fact, it's been said we most effectively love ourselves by loving God and others because this is how we are made to thrive and find meaning in life. We must do what is needed to gain a deeper understanding and appreciation for how these primary relationships work and where we still struggle to line up with God and others. Even in day-to-day operations, we need an ongoing commitment to excellence. After all, 2 Corinthians 5:20 says we are to be "Ambassadors for Christ" on this earth. That's the bottom line and the underlying theme of this series.

CREATION INVITES CREATIVITY

One more story: going back to when I first heard the Good News, I remember being so inspired by the idea that God hadn't just set up shop, created everything, and then moved on to something more important. I think we tend to have that idea before we really get into the Word and see how intimately and intricately involved He truly is in every aspect of His creation and our lives. This theme of ongoing commitment has stayed with me through the many businesses I've taken on to discover, develop, and deploy, and it's helped me stay focused on what's most important when things aren't going as well as I'd like, or are starting to look like they're coming off the rails. You'd be crazy to think you're not going to have those days—or weeks, or even months.

In fact, when you're just starting out with these concepts, it can take some time to get the ideas and pieces to line up. Don't get disappointed if your vision isn't matching up with reality even 12-18 months out. Most people will give up before they see results in any business. But if you've followed these steps and worked to apply them both to yourself and your business, I believe there's nothing you will face in God's strength and care that will derail His call in your life. Continuing to work toward refining the relationships, momentum, order, structure, culture, and vision as you encounter challenges is how you'll come to dominate the market for the Kingdom.

Every snag in the operation is an opportunity to adjust for greater growth. The question is often, *How far back do we need to go to truly deal with and eradicate this problem effectively?* That's where creativity comes in.

God's word contains creative power. As beings created in his image, we have been given that power as well. Using it when needed, and activating that gift responsibly for the good of our businesses, but ultimately for the advancing of the Kingdom, is how prepared Kingdom Entrepreneurs can come to establish dominion and encourage our world to flourish. While Day Seven is a reminder to demonstrate proper honor to God *for* the work and creativity He's provided, every day is a chance to honor and be with God *in* the work, and dedicate our progress and fulfillment in it to Him.

Does an employee have the drive but needs better training to effectively identify better leads or inspire clients to sign on? What resources can you mobilize to provide that? Does a supplier need a bigger vision for creating the specific part to give your product a competitive advantage? How can you strategically inspire and motivate the owner or encourage them to see their importance to your bottom line?

Creativity is a God-given power each of us can activate to solve problems and refine our businesses. The efforts you apply to creatively shape your business's vision, culture, structure, order, and movement make it effective and appealing like a well-tended garden or a polished machine. Creative investment all along that chain has a massive quality impact as well. The greater relationship power your business ultimately creates will be largely dependent on those efforts to tweak and edit your processes on the front end.

APPLY CONSISTENT EFFORT

After reading all the stories and ideas here, the question for you now is, *How will you use this in real life?* It's in the real-life application that you'll come to see the real value of these principles. Then, as these ideas take root and you get your business running, what will keep you going when you see trouble crop up and things breaking down?

There's an old illustration about how a single drop of water can eventually break through stone if it continues consistently. The point is clear: it's not about strength or force, but consistency and determination. Remember Rocky and so many other movies and stories about people who overcame the odds through the power of their commitment. Even better, our ultimate example went to the Cross for what He believed in—that we could have eternal life with Him someday if only He'd make the way someday. Like the old song says, "Nobody knew his secret ambition," but we can know that our connection to Him fuels our commitment and supplies all we need to remember when we face any struggle in life.

1 Peter 4:11 says, "Whoever speaks *is to do so* as *one who is speaking* actual words of God; whoever serves *is to do so* as *one who is serving* by the strength which God supplies; so that in all things God may be glorified through Jesus Christ, to whom belongs the glory and dominion forever and ever. Amen." I can think of no more fitting words to encourage all of us. We are the Kingdom creatives who get to take this work forward in the power of the name of the One who commands the very waves. Think about that next time you find yourself forgetting what really matters. Pray with persistence and work with an awareness of this promise. The only real limitation we have is our appreciation of this empowering truth.

Whatever we do, when we are properly aligned with Him and His call, we speak and serve in as those conveying the very words of God. The work, the real work, is becoming properly aligned to activate this kind of infinite power and grace.

It's in that knowledge of your real mission I pray you'll feel prepared and fully capable of meeting the challenges that will come to test and mold you in the work you've been assigned. May God bless the work of your hands, and may it bring great glory to the King.

To Learn More About
The King's Council or to
Join The Community Go To:

https://kingscouncilcommunity.org/

RYLEE MEEK

To Learn More About
Rylee Meek Go To:

www.ryleemeek.com

Be sure to check out the second & third books in the

Kingdom Entrepreneur Series

Book 3 coming from Rylee Meek and The King's Council in 2024!

Listen to the King's Council Podcast

New Episodes Every Thursday

The King's Council Podcast is designed to equip you with the tools necessary to discover, develop, and deploy your God given vision into the marketplace. We believe God's greatest gift to us is life, therefore our greatest gift to Him is what we do with it. This is why, each week, Rylee Meek will bring to you new insights, based on the foundational truths taught throughout the Bible. All of our teaching, coaching, and ministry is rooted in and flows out of these biblical doctrines. www.ryleemeek.com/podcast

Made in the USA
Middletown, DE
20 March 2024

51265165R00075